The Sayings of Shakespeare

The Sayings series

Jane Austen
Charlotte Brontë
Lord Byron
Lewis Carroll
Winston Churchill
Charles Dickens
Benjamin Disraeli
F. Scott Fitzgerald
Benjamin Franklin
Goethe
Thomas Hardy
Henrik Ibsen
Dr Johnson
James Joyce
John Keats
Rudyard Kipling
D.H. Lawrence
Somerset Maugham
Friedrich Nietzsche
George Orwell
Dorothy Parker
Samuel Pepys
Ezra Pound
Sir Walter Scott
William Shakespeare
George Bernard Shaw
Sydney Smith
R.L. Stevenson
Jonathan Swift
Leo Tolstoy
Anthony Trollope
Mark Twain
Evelyn Waugh
Oscar Wilde
Virginia Woolf
W.B. Yeats
The Bible
The Buddha
Jesus
Moses
Muhammad

The Sayings of

SHAKESPEARE

edited by

A.L. ROWSE

DUCKWORTH

Third impression 1997
Second impression September 1993
First published in March 1993 by
Gerald Duckworth & Co. Ltd.
The Old Piano Factory
48 Hoxton Square, London N1 6PB
Tel: 0171 729 5986
Fax: 0171 729 0015

Introduction and editorial arrangement
© 1993 by A.L. Rowse

A catalogue record for this book is available
from the British Library

ISBN 0 7156 2458 X

Typeset by Ray Davies
Printed in Great Britain by
Redwood Books Ltd, Trowbridge

Contents

7   Introduction

11   On Himself

14   Poetry

16   Love

20   Women

23   Music

25   Acting & the Stage

29   Society & Politics

36   Monarchy & the Court

38   England

40   Virtues & Vices

45   Everyday Remarks

48   Characteristic Reflections

63   Religion

To

Margaret Thatcher

Historic Figure, English Patriot

Introduction

A common misconception about William Shakespeare is to say that we know little about him, and there are people so ignorant as to call him 'anonymous'. This only means that *they* don't know. The truth is that we know more about him than about any other dramatist of the Elizabethan age, when theatre folk were not written up. And all that we know about him from external evidence is completely consistent with the internal evidence from his own work. So that – quite contrary to popular misunderstanding – we are on firm ground with our knowledge of him.

Again it is hardly yet realised that he was the most autobiographical of those dramatists. He tells us a great deal about himself and about the life of his time, but it needs an intimate knowledge of that time, four hundred years ago, to catch and interpret all the references to it, the events, the social life, the tone and temper of the age. His was in fact a candid, truth-telling spirit, though often his manner of expressing himself was prudently indirect as he himself recommends, by 'indirections to find directions out'. He was a prudent, tactful, courteous gentleman, who regularly recommends discretion – one of the few theatre people who never got into trouble. A subtle mind, a very clever man – it stands to reason that most of what has been written about him is not only not on the level of the subject, but by people who, without the knowledge or perception, do not qualify to express an opinion. Safer to ignore them, and read, see and hear Shakespeare himself.

In reading what he wrote, his own sayings, we are taken straight into the mind and heart of the man he was. Here we are not illustrating the marvellous dramatist – the world's greatest, when all is considered – or the poet, supreme master of our language, but the thoughts that welled up in his mind. And naturally, as with any of us, they are more revealing of the man.

Yet here again there is a further subtlety to encounter

with a dramatist. Sometimes, in accordance with the characters speaking, he appears to say opposed things – with regard to conscience, for example, or men's attitude to death. We need not think of these as contradictions. Not only do characters in plays think different things, but often we do ourselves, and not only at different times of life. But when Shakespeare enforces an opinion unvaryingly, several times over – against ingratitude, envy, even drunkenness – we may be sure that they represent something special to him.

What astonishes one in this self-portrayal of his mind is that he seems to have understood everyone and everything, every character and kind of human being. And no less astonishing that he had no illusions – not even about himself: we know that from the Sonnets, the most autobiographical and candid ever written. He had an enormous advantage here as a theatre man, as an actor himself, in putting himself into the minds and feelings of other characters, women as well as men. Hence his repeated observations about the contrast between seeming and being. A clever old man once said in my hearing, 'I love the duplicity in things.' William Shakespeare might well have said that – no one ever understood their ambivalence, the two-sidedness, the rainbow-like changeability, better than he did.

At the same time his view of society is firmly grounded in the governing opinion of his age, the paramount necessity of preserving social order. For his, like ours, was an age of ideological – they called it religious – conflict. Neighbouring France, the Netherlands, Scotland were torn by civil war, as England and Ireland were soon to be. William Shakespeare was a patriot, a countryman with the love of countryside and country sports, but he had no love of war and fighting any more than his great creation Sir John Falstaff had. His sympathies were conservative of society, with the old faith – an old-style Anglican – and old ways. He saw through both sides, a fig for Opinion, and that the crust of civilisation is indeed thin: break through it, and what dark waters men plunge into. We have seen that appallingly confirmed in our own time. Liberal illusions about the masses do not save them from slaughter and homicide.

Shakespeare's understanding of society, the necessities, hypocrisies, cruelties of politics – deeper and more to the point than all the other dramatists of his time – it is here that the urgencies of our own time have given us a clearer conception than before. We might note this as our chief contribution to Shakespeare 'criticism', if the word may be permitted. Hence this provides a full section here.

In his own time, as a poet he was known as the poet of love, the English Ovid. Another, even fuller, section illustrates this. His exposure of the realities and dangers, the urgencies of society and government, is tempered by an extraordinary humaneness, like those other best spirits of the age, Montaigne and Cervantes, congenial to him. Their sceptical temper was not taken in by anything, they saw through it. It comes through as something of a surprise what a moralist Shakespeare was – as much as his great critic, Dr Johnson – not only in his observations on every class and type of men and women, from rulers to peasants, mechanics and criminals, but in the remarks he makes, often conclusions, as to conduct and behaviour. This thus provides the two longest sections of his sayings and comments on us, humanity in general.

Impossible to illustrate all his tastes – for country sports, deer-hunting, bowls, falconry, archery – they were gentlemanly, upper-class. He was not one for bumbling about the town, or for the shady company of literary Bohemia, unlike Robert Greene (who attacked him for being up-stage) or poor Christopher Marlowe (whose genius he generously appreciated). He preferred the society of his patron, a young Earl.

I have seen him described as 'unmusical' (how much sillier can one be?). He was the most musical of all the Elizabethan writers. He loved music, and he adored women – interesting to see here that he related the two.

It is significant that the shortest section is that on religion. This is not just because discussion of the subject was prohibited on the Elizabethan stage, for it led to bloodshed. Shakespeare was not interested in discussion of the subject (as Marlowe was). This was not because he was not a religious man (as Marlowe was not); but because he clearly thought that one could not box up the mystery of the universe and of our status in it, human life, in the confines of dogma, abstract propositions.

He evidently thought little of them: so much of his thinking is concrete, realist, imaginative, in striking, recognisable images. All the more convincing and true for that. Once more, a sceptical man, like Montaigne, thought that the best position, or solution, if you like, was acceptance, to conform – not to question or to challenge, as if one could penetrate the mystery. 'Hang up philosophy!'

The universe of human nature is what we *can* know about, in all its variety and manifestations, good as well as evil. For him it was all in all, indeed enough.

Authorities

William Shakespeare, The Complete Works, ed. by C.J. Sisson. I prefer this text, since Sisson was familiar with colloquial Elizabethan English from intimate knowledge of documents, like an historian. Since it is out of print, next best is the standard edition of Peter Alexander.

For elucidation of archaic words and phrases my edition, *The Contemporary Shakespeare*, pub. by the University Press of America, 4720 Boston Way, Lanham, Maryland, USA 20706. For biography, information as to contemporary references in the Plays, etc, my *Shakespeare the Man; Prefaces to Shakespeare's Plays; Shakespeare's Self-Portrait*. Mark Eccles: *Shakespeare in Warwickshire*.

For background, my *The England of Elizabeth I; The Elizabethan Renaissance*, vol. 2, *The Cultural Achievement*. E.K. Chambers: *The Elizabethan Stage*, 4 vols. G.E. Bentley: *The Jacobean and Caroline Stage*, 2 vols.

For 'Criticism': Granville Barker, *Prefaces to Shakespeare's Plays*, 3 vols.

On Himself

Yet writers say, as in the sweetest bud
The eating canker dwells, so eating love
Inhabits in the finest wits of all.

The Two Gentlemen of Verona, I.1

To be in love, where scorn is bought with groans,
Coy looks with heart-sore sighs, one fading moment's
  mirth,
With twenty, watchful, weary, tedious nights,
If haply won, perhaps a hapless gain,
If lost, why then a grievous labour won –
However, but a folly bought with wit,
Or else a wit by folly vanquishèd.

Ibid

A merrier man –
Within the limit of becoming mirth –
I never spent an hoür's talk withal.
His eye begets occasion for his wit,
For every object that the one doth catch
The other turns to a mirth-moving jest.

Love's Labour's Lost, II.1

Let those who are in favour with their stars
Of public honour and proud titles boast,
Whilst I, whom fortune of such triumph bars,
Unlooked for joy in that I honour most.

Sonnet 25

a discontented gentleman
Whose humble means match not his haughty mind.

Richard III, IV.2

Thy love is better than high birth to me,
Richer than wealth, prouder than garments' cost,
Of more delight than hawks or horses be.　　Sonnet 91

Never believe, though in my nature reigned
All frailties that besiege all kinds of blood,
That it could so preposterously be stained
To leave for nothing all thy sum of good.　　Sonnet 109

Alas, 'tis true, I have gone here and there
And made myself a motley to the view,
Gored mine own thoughts, sold cheap what is most dear.
　　　　　　　　　　　　　　　　　Sonnet 110

O, for my sake do you with Fortune chide,
The guilty goddess of my harmful deeds,
That did not better for my life provide
Than public means, which public manners breeds.
　　　　　　　　　　　　　　　　　Sonnet 111

'Tis better to be vile than vile esteemed,
When not to be receives reproach of being,
And the just pleasure lost, which is so deemed –
Not by our feeling – but by others' seeing.
　　　　　　　　　　　　　　　　　Sonnet 121

For why should others' false adulterate eyes
Give salutation to my sportive blood?
Or on my frailties why are frailer spies,
Which in their wills count bad what I think good?
　　　　　　　　　　　　　　　　　　Ibid

No, I am that I am, and they that level
At my abuses reckon up their own:
I may be straight, though they themselves be bevel.
　　　　　　　　　　　　　　　　　　Ibid

They say best men are moulded out of faults
And, for the most part, become much more the better
For being a little bad.

Measure for Measure, V.1

The expense of spirit in a waste of shame
Is lust in action ...
Enjoyed no sooner but despisèd straight,
Past reason hunted, and no sooner had
Past reason hated as a swallowed bait
On purpose laid to make the taker mad ...

Sonnet 129

He is complete in feature and in mind
With all good grace to grace a gentleman.

As You Like It, I.1

In my youth I never did apply
Hot and rebellious liquors in my blood.

Ibid, II.3

I hate ingratitude more in a man
Than lying, vainness, babbling drunkenness.

Twelfth Night, III.4

For mine own part I could be well content
To entertain the lag-end of my life
With quiet hours.

1 King Henry IV, V.1

In Nature's infinite book of secrecy
A little can I read.

Antony and Cleopatra, I.2

Poetry

Our poesy is as a gum which oozes
From whence 'tis nourished ...

Timon of Athens, I.1

Much is the force of heaven-bred poesy.

The Two Gentlemen of Verona, III.2

The poet's eye, in a fine frenzy rolling,
Doth glance from heaven to earth, from earth to heaven,
And as imagination bodies forth
The forms of things unknown, the poet's pen
Turns them to shapes, and gives to airy nothing
A local habitation and a name.

A Midsummer Night's Dream, V.1

Never durst poet touch a pen to write
Until his ink were tempered with love's sighs.

Love's Labour's Lost, IV.2

Let me supervise the canzonet. Here are only numbers
ratified; but for the elegance, facility, and golden
cadence of poetry – *caret* [it is wanting].

Ibid

Did you hear these verses?
 – Some of them had in them more feet than the verses
would bear.

As You Like It, III.2

God be with you, if you
talk in blank verse.

Ibid, IV.1

Why is my verse so barren of new pride,
So far from variation or quick change?
Why with the time do I not glance aside
To new-found methods and to compounds strange?

Sonnet 76

Why write I still all one, ever the same ...
That every word doth almost tell my name?

Ibid

Then do thy office, Muse: I teach thee how
To make him seem long hence as he shows now.

Sonnet 101

... all alike my songs and praises be
To one, of one, still such and ever so.

Sonnet 105

So have I invoked thee for my Muse ...
As every alien pen hath got my use
And under thee their poesy disperse.

Sonnet 78

I had rather be a kitten and cry mew
Than one of these same metre ballad-mongers.

1 King Henry IV, III.1

Love

Friendship is constant in all other things
Save in the office and affairs of love.

Much Ado About Nothing, II.1

O spirit of love! how quick and fresh art thou.

Twelfth Night, I.1

What is love? 'Tis not hereafter …
  What's to come is still unsure.
In delay there lies no plenty …
  Youth's a stuff will not endure.

Ibid, II.3

But love, first learnèd in a lady's eyes,
Lives not alone immurèd in the brain,
But with the motion of all elements
Courses as swift as thought in every power,
And gives to every power a double power.

Love's Labour's Lost, IV.3

Alas that love, so gentle in his view,
Should be so tyrannous and rough in proof!

Romeo and Juliet, I.1

This is the monstruosity in love – that the will is infinite
and the execution confined, that the desire is boundless
and the act a slave to limit.

Troilus and Cressida, III.2

To be wise and love
Exceeds man's might.

Ibid

Therefore love moderately – long love doth so,
Too swift arrives as tardy as too slow.

Romeo and Juliet, II.6

If thou rememberest not the slightest folly
That ever love did make thee run into
Thou hast not loved.

As You like It, II.4

We that are true lovers run into strange capers.

Ibid

Prosperity's the very bond of love,
Whose fresh complexion and whose heart together
Affliction alters.

The Winter's Tale, IV.3

When love begins to sicken and decay
It useth an enforcèd ceremony.

Julius Caesar, IV.2

Some men must love my lady, some Joan.

Love's Labour's Lost, III.1

The ostentation of our love which unshown
Is often left unloved.

Antony and Cleopatra, III.6

Dead shepherd, now I find thy saw of might:
'Who ever loved that loved not at first sight?'

As You Like It, III.5

Men have died from time to time, and worms have eaten them – but not for love.

Ibid, IV.1

Love is not love
When it is mingled with regards that stand
Aloof from the main point.

King Lear, I.1

All true lovers are
Unstaid and skittish in all motions else
Save in the constant image of the creature
That is beloved.

Twelfth Night, II.4

Not so young to love a woman for singing, nor so old to dote on her for anything.

King Lear, I.4

The course of true love never did run smooth.

A Midsummer Night's Dream, I.2

Love looks not with the eyes but with the mind.

Ibid

Men were deceivers ever –
One foot in sea, and one on shore,
To one thing constant never.

Much Ado About Nothing, I.3

Doth not the appetite alter? A man loves the meat in his youth that he cannot endure in his age.

Ibid, II.1

Love sought is good, but given unsought is better.
Twelfth Night, III.1

What damnèd minutes tells he o'er
Who dotes yet doubts – suspects yet soundly loves!
Othello, III.3

All lovers young, all lovers must
Consign to thee and come to dust.
Cymbeline, IV.2

Love is not love
Which alters when it alteration finds,
Or bends with the remover to remove.
Sonnet 116

But love is blind, and lovers cannot see
The pretty follies that themselves commit.
The Merchant of Venice, II.2

Women

Do you not know I am a woman? What I think I must speak.
As You Like It, III.2

A very honest woman, but something given to lie.
Antony and Cleopatra, V.2

I know that a woman is a dish for the gods, if the devil dress her not.
Ibid

How hard it is for women to keep counsel!
Julius Caesar, II.4

There was never yet fair woman but she made mouths in a glass.
King Lear, III.2

> Her voice was ever soft,
> Gentle and low, an excellent thing in woman.
Ibid, V.3

From women's eyes this doctrine I derive:
They sparkle still the right Promethean fire,
They are the books, the arts, the academes,
That show, contain and nourish all the world.
Love's Labour's Lost, IV.3

For where is any author in the world
Teaches such beauty as a woman's eye?
Ibid

Black brows, they say,
Become some women best, so that there be not
Too much hair there, but in a semi-circle
Or a half-moon made with a pen.
The Winter's Tale, II.1

A light wife doth make a heavy husband.
The Merchant of Venice, V.1

Cupid is a knavish lad
Thus to make poor females mad.
A Midsummer Night's Dream, III.2

Wooing, wedding, and repenting is as a Scotch jig, a
measure, and a cinque-pace [quick dance].
Much Ado About Nothing, I.1

Would it not grieve a woman to be over-mastered with a
piece of valiant dust? to make an account of her life to a
clod of wayward marl? *Ibid*, II.1

She is a woman, therefore may be wooed,
She is a woman, therefore may be won.
Titus Andronicus, II.1

Women are angels, wooing;
Things won are done, joy's soul lies in the doing.
That she beloved knows naught that knows not this:
Men prize the thing ungained more than it is.
Troilus and Cressida, I.1

Is there no way for men to be, but women
Must be half-workers?
Cymbeline, II.5

Let still [ever] the woman take
An elder to herself, so wears she to him
So sways she level in her husband's heart ...
Our fancies are more giddy and unfirm,
More longing, wavering, sooner lost and worn,
Than women's are.   *Twelfth Night*, II.4

Constant you are,
But yet a woman; and for secrecy
No lady closer – for I well believe
Thou wilt not utter what thou dost not know.
                    1 King Henry IV, II.3

Maids are May when they are maids, but the sky
changes when they are wives.   *As You Like It*, IV.1

Down on your knees,
And thank heaven, fasting, for a good man's love.
                    Ibid, III.5

Thy husband is thy lord, thy life, thy keeper,
Thy head, thy sovereign; one that cares for thee,
And for thy maintenance commits his body
To painful labour both by sea and land,
To watch the night in storms, the day in cold,
Whilst thou liest warm at home, secure and safe;
And craves no other tribute at his hands
But love, fair looks, and true obedience.
                    The Taming of the Shrew, V.2

I am ashamed that women are so simple
To offer war where they should kneel for peace.
                    Ibid

A woman moved is like a fountain troubled,
Muddy, ill-seeming, thick, bereft of beauty.   *Ibid*

Music

In sweet music is such art
Killing care and grief of heart.
King Henry VIII, III.1

Music: moody food of us that trade in love.
Antony and Cleopatra, II.5

Music oft hath such a charm
To make bad good, and good provoke to harm.
Measure for Measure, IV.1

Loud music is too harsh for ladies' heads.
Pericles, II.3

Music and poesy use to quicken you.
The Taming of the Shrew, I.1

Music with her silver sound
With speedy help doth lend redress.
Romeo and Juliet, IV.5

How sour sweet music is
When time is broke and no proportion kept!
King Richard II, V.5

The man that hath no music in himself,
Nor is not moved with concord of sweet sounds,
Is fit for treasons, stratagems, and spoils.
The Merchant of Venice, V.1

Music to hear, why hear'st thou music sadly? ...
Why lov'st thou that which thou receiv'st not gladly? ...
Mark how one string, sweet husband to another,
Strikes each in each by mutual ordering.

Sonnet 8

That old and antique song we heard last night
Methought it did relieve my passion much
More than light airs.

Twelfth Night, II.4

Visit by night your lady's chamber window
With some sweet consort. To their instruments
Tune a deploring dump.

The Two Gentlemen of Verona, III.2

Is it not strange that sheep's guts should hale souls out
of men's bodies?

Much Ado About Nothing, I.3

Bare, ruined choirs where late the sweet birds sang.

Sonnet 73

Acting & the Stage

How many ages hence
Shall this our lofty scene be acted over
In states unborn, and accents yet unknown?

Julius Caesar, III.1

All the world's a stage,
And all the men and women merely players;
They have their exits and their entrances
And one man in his time plays many parts,
His acts being seven ages.

As You Like It, II.7

'Tis ten to one this play can never please
All that are here. Some come to take their ease
And sleep an act or two …
So 'tis clear
They'll say 'tis naught.

King Henry VIII, Epilogue

Now the play is done –
All is well ended if this suit be won
That you express content: which we will pay
With strife to please you, day exceeding day.

All's Well That Ends Well, Epilogue

These our actors,
As I foretold you, were all spirits and
Are melted into air …
We are such stuff
As dreams are made on, and our little life
Is rounded with a sleep.

The Tempest, IV.1

As in a theatre the eyes of men,
After a well-graced actor leaves the stage,
Are idly bent on him that enters next,
Thinking his prattle to be tedious.   *King Richard II*, V.2

As an unperfect actor on the stage
Who with his fear is put beside his part,
Or some fierce thing replete with too much rage
Whose strength's abundance weakens his own heart.

Sonnet 23

Like a strutting player, whose conceit
Lies in his hamstring, and doth think it rich
To hear the wooden dialogue and sound
'Twixt his stretched footing and the scaffoldage.

Troilus and Cressida, I.3

Speak the speech, I pray you, as I pronounced it to you –
trippingly on the tongue. But if you mouth it, as many of
your players do, I had as lief the town-crier spake my
lines.   *Hamlet*, III.1

Nor do not saw the air too much with your hand – thus
... Be not too tame neither ... Suit the action to the word,
the word to the action. With this special observance –
that you o'er-step not the modesty of nature. For
anything so overdone is from the purpose of playing –
whose end, both at the first and now was and is, to hold
(as 'twere) the mirror up to nature.   *Ibid*

And let those that play your clowns speak no more than
is set down for them. For there be of them that will
themselves laugh, to set on some quantity of barren
spectators to laugh too – though in the meantime some
necessary question of the play be then to be considered.
That's villainous, and shows a most pitiful ambition in
the fool that uses it.   *Ibid*, III.2

I have thought some of nature's journeymen had made
men, and not made them well, they imitated humanity
so abominably.

Ibid, II.1

And if the boy have not a woman's gift
To rain a shower of commanded tears,
An onion will do well for such a shift –
Which in a napkin being close conveyed
Shall in despite enforce a watering eye.

The Taming of the Shrew, Induction 1

You make faces like mummers.   *Coriolanus,* II.1

Pat he comes like catastrophe in the old comedy. My cue
is villainous melancholy.

King Lear, I.2

He doth it as like one of these harlotry players as ever I
see.

1 King Henry IV, II.4

Is it not monstrous that this player here,
But in a fiction, in a dream of passion,
Could force his soul so to his own conceit
That from her working all his visage wanned –
Tears in his eyes, distraction in his aspect
A broken voice ...
          And all for nothing!

Hamlet, II.2

          Is there no play
To ease the anguish of a torturing hour?

A Midsummer Night's Dream, V.1

This green plot shall be our stage, this hawthorn-brake
our tiring-house.

Ibid, III.1

The best in this kind are but shadows, and the worst are
no worse, if imagination amend them.

Ibid, V.1

Guilty creatures sitting at a play
Have by the very cunning of the scene
Been struck so to the soul that presently
They have proclaimed their malefactions.

Hamlet, II.2

The play pleased not the million, 'twas caviare to the
general.

Ibid

[The purpose of playing] To show ... the very age and
body of the time his form and pressure.

Ibid

Will you see the players well bestowed? Do you hear, let
them be well used; for they are the abstracts and brief
chronicles of the time. After your death you were better
have a bad epitaph than their ill report while you live.

Ibid

Life's but a walking shadow, a poor player
That struts and frets his hour upon the stage
And then is heard no more.

Macbeth, V.5

Society & Politics

There is a mystery – with whom relation
Durst never meddle – in the soul of state,
Which hath an operation more divine
Than breath or pen can give expressure to.
Troilus and Cressida, III.3

The heavens themselves, the planets, and this centre
Observe degree, priority, and place,
Insisture, course, proportion, season, form,
Office and custom, all in line of order.

Ibid, I.3

      O, when degree is shaked,
Which is the ladder to all high designs,
The enterprise is sick.   *Ibid*

      How could communities,
Degrees in schools, and brotherhoods in cities,
Peaceful commerce from dividable shores,
The primogenitive and due of birth,
Prerogative of age, crowns, sceptres, laurels,
But by degree stand in authentic place?   *Ibid*

Take but degree away, untune that string,
And hark what discord follows ...
Strength should be lord of imbecility [weakness],
Force should be right; or rather, right and wrong
Should lose their names, and so should justice too.
Then everything includes itself in power,
Power into will, will into appetite,
And appetite – a universal wolf –
Must make perforce a universal prey
And last eat up himself.   *Ibid*

[Shakespeare's ironical account of Communism]:
In the commonwealth I would by contraries
Execute all things …
                    no name of magistrate;
Letters should not be known; riches, poverty,
And use of service, none; contract, succession,
Bourn, bound of land, tilth, vineyard, none;
No use of metal, corn, or wine, or oil;
No occupation. All men idle, all.
And women too, but innocent and pure.
No sovereignty …

[He continues contemptuously]:
All things in common nature should produce
Without sweat or endeavour. Treason, felony,
Sword, pike, knife, gun, or need of any engine,
Would I not have. But nature should bring forth,
Of its own kind, all foison [harvest], all abundance,
To feed my innocent people.

[Someone asks]:
No marrying among his subjects?
– None, man. All idle, whores and knaves.

The Tempest, II.1

They well deserve to have
That know the surest way to get.

King Richard II, III.3

From lowest place when virtuous things proceed
The place is dignified by the doer's deed.
Where great additions swell us, and virtue none,
It is a dropsied honour …
The property by what it is should go,
Not by the title.

All's Well That Ends Well, II.3

Honours thrive
When rather from our note we them derive
Than our foregoers. The mere word's a slave.

Ibid

O place! O form!
How often dost thou with thy case, thy habit,
Wrench awe from fools, and tie the wiser souls
To thy false seeming.

Measure for Measure, II.4

O place and greatness! Millions of false eyes
Are stuck upon thee; volumes of report
Run with these false and most contrarious quests
Upon thy doings.

Ibid, IV.1

No might nor greatness in mortality
Can censure 'scape; back-wounding calumny
The whitest virtue strikes. What king so strong
Can tie the gall up in the slanderous tongue?

Ibid, III.2

What great ones do the less will prattle of.

Twelfth Night, I.2

That smooth-faced gentleman, tickling Commodity,
[Convenience]
Commodity, the bias of the world;
The world, who of itself is peizèd [poised] well ...
Till this advantage, this vile-drawing bias ...
Makes it take head from all indifferency [impartiality]
From all direction, purpose, course, intent.

King John, II.1

Get thee glass eyes,
And, like a scurvy politician, seem
To see the thing thou dost not.

King Lear, IV.6

O world, thy slippery turns! Friends now fast sworn ...
Unseparable, shall within this hour,
On a dissension of a doit, break out
To bitterest enmity. So fellest foes,
Whose passions and whose plots have broke their sleep
...
By some trick not worth an egg, shall grow dear friends.

Coriolanus, IV.4

Men, like butterflies,
Show not their mealy wings but to the summer;
And not a man, for being simply man,
Hath any honour, but honour for those honours
That are without him, as places, riches, and favour,
Prizes of accident as oft as merit.

Troilus and Cressida, III.3

'Tis certain greatness, once fallen out with fortune
Must fall out with men too: what the declined is
He shall as soon read in the eyes of others
As feel in his own fall.

Ibid

The great man down you mark his favourite flies,
The poor advanced makes friends of enemies.
And hitherto doth love on fortune tend;
For who not needs shall never lack a friend,
And who in want a hollow friend doth try
Directly seasons him his enemy.

Hamlet, III.2

Men shut their doors against a setting sun.

Timon of Athens, I.2

The general's disdained
By him one step below, he by the next,
That next by him beneath. So every step,
Exampled by the first pace that is sick
Of his superior, grows to an envious fever
Of pale and bloodless emulation [envy].

Troilus and Cressida, I.3

Policy I hate. I'd as lief be a Brownist [Puritan] as a
politician.

Twelfth Night, III.2

Where gentry, title, wisdom
Cannot conclude but by the Yea and No
Of general ignorance, it must omit
Real necessities ...
       Purpose so barred, it follows
Nothing is done to purpose.

Coriolanus, III.1

The multitudinous tongue – let them not lick
The sweet which is their poison. Your dishonour
Mangles true judgment and bereaves the state
Of that integrity which should become it –
Not having the power to do the good it would
For the ill which doth control it.

Ibid

Our slippery people
Whose love is never linked to the deserver
Till his deserts are passed.

Antony and Cleopatra, I.2

An habitation giddy and unsure
Hath he that buildeth on the vulgar heart.

2 King Henry IV, I.3

And that's the wavering commons, for their love
Lies in their purses, and who empties them
By so much fills their hearts with deadly hate.

King Richard II, II.2

And manhood is called foolery when it stands
Against a falling fabric.

Coriolanus, III.1

There have been many great men that have flattered the
people, who ne'er loved them; and there be many that
they have loved, they know not wherefore. So that if
they love they know not why, they hate upon no better a
ground.

Ibid, II.1

He which is was wished until he were,
And the ebbed man, ne'er loved till ne'er worth love,
Comes deared by being lacked.

Antony and Cleopatra, I.4

Authority, though it err like others,
Hath yet a kind of medicine in itself.

Measure for Measure, II.2.

The pate of a politician – one that could circumvent God.

Hamlet, V.1

Yet he that can endure
To follow with allegiance a fallen lord
Does conquer him that did his master conquer.

Antony and Cleopatra, III.11

They tax our policy and call it cowardice,
Count wisdom as no member of the war,
Forestall prescience, and esteem no act
But that of hand.

Troilus and Cressida, I.3

The still and mental parts
That do contrive how many hands shall strike,
When fitness calls them on, and know by measure
Of their observant toil the enemies' weight ...
They call this bed-work, mappery, closet-war.

Ibid

Since every Jack became a gentleman
There's many a gentle person made a Jack.

King Richard III, I.3

'Tis better to be lowly born
And range with humble livers in content
Than to be perked up in a glistering grief,
And wear a golden sorrow.

King Henry VIII, II.3

Let me be no assistant for a state
But keep a farm and carters.

Hamlet, II.2

Monarchy & the Court

Not all the water in the rough, rude sea
Can wash the balm from an anointed king.

King Richard II, III.2

Princes have but their titles for their glories,
An outward honour for an inward toil ...
They often feel a world of restless cares.
So that between their titles, and low name,
There's nothing differs but the outward fame.

King Richard III, I.4

What infinite heart's ease
Must kings neglect that private men enjoy!
And what have kings that privates have not too
Save ceremony, save general ceremony?

King Henry V, IV.1

Uneasy lies the head that wears a crown.

2 King Henry IV, III.1

O ceremony, show me but thy worth ...
Art thou aught else but place, degree, and form,
Creating awe and fear in other men?

King Henry V, IV.1

Like vassalage at unawares encountering
The eye of majesty.

Troilus and Cressida, III.2

The Court's a learning place.

All's Well That Ends Well, I.1

The art of the Court –
As hard to leave as keep – whose top to climb
Is certain falling, or so slippery that
The fear's as bad as falling.   *Cymbeline*, III.3

Not a courtier –
Although they wear their faces to the bent
Of the king's looks – hath a heart that is not
Glad at the thing they scowl at.   *Ibid*, I.1

If God have lent a man any manners he may easily put it
off at Court. He that cannot make a leg [curtsey], put off
his cap, kiss his hand, and say nothing, has neither leg,
hands, lip, nor cap. And indeed, such a fellow, to say
precisely, were not for the Court.
                    All's Well That Ends Well, II.2

A courtier ... could say, 'Good morrow, sweet lord!
How dost thou, good lord?' This might be my Lord
Such-a-one, that praised my Lord Such-a-one's horse,
when he meant to beg it.   *Hamlet*, V.1

Those that are good manners at the Court are as
ridiculous in the country as the behaviour in the country
is most mockable at the Court. You salute not at the
Court but you kiss your hands; that courtesy would be
uncleanly if courtiers were shepherds. The courtier's
hands are perfumed with civet.   *As You Like It*, III.2

Hath not old custom made this life more sweet
Than those of painted pomp? Are not these woods
More free from peril than the envious Court?
                    Ibid, II.1

Lord, who would live turmoiled in the Court,
And may enjoy such quiet walks as these?
This small inheritance my father left me
Contenteth me, and worth a monarchy.
                    2 King Henry VI, IV.10

England

This fortress built by nature for herself
Against infection and the hand of war,
This happy breed of men, this little world,
This precious stone set in the silver sea ...
This blessèd plot, this earth, this realm, this England.

King Richard II, II.1

This England never did, nor never shall,
Lie at the proud foot of a conqueror,
But when it first did help to wound itself.

King John, V.7

Our countrymen ...
Now wingèd, with their courage will make known
To their approvers they are people such
That mend upon the world.

Cymbeline, II.4

And gentlemen in England now a-bed
Shall think themselves accursed they were not here,
And hold their manhoods cheap while any speaks
That fought with us upon St Crispin's day.

King Henry V, IV.3

Good yeomen,
Whose limbs were made in England, show us here
The mettle of your pasture.

Ibid, III.1

O England, model to thy inward greatness –
Like little body with a mighty heart
What might thou do, that honour would thee do,
Were all thy children kind and natural.

Ibid, I.2

The natural bravery of your isle, which stands
As Neptune's park, ribbed and palèd in
With rocks unscalable and roaring waters.

Cymbeline, III.1

Hath Britain all the sun that shines?

Ibid, III.4

It was always yet the trick of our English nation – if they
have a good thing to make it too common.

2 King Henry IV, I.2

Why was he sent into England?
– Why, because he was mad. He shall recover his wits
there; or, if he do not, 'tis no great matter there.

Hamlet, V.1

Virtues & Vices

Lord, what fools these mortals be!

A Midsummer Night's Dream, III.2

All things that are
Are with more spirit chasèd than enjoyed.

The Merchant of Venice, II.6

They that have power to hurt and will do none,
That do not do the thing they most do show,
Who, moving others, are themselves as stone,
Unmovèd, cold and to temptation slow ...
They are the lords and owners of their faces.

Sonnet 94

Time hath ... a wallet at his back,
Wherein he puts alms for oblivion,
A great-sized monster of ingratitudes:
Those scraps are good deeds past, which are devoured
As fast as they are made, forgot as soon.

Troilus and Cressida, III.3

There's no art
To find the mind's construction in the face.

Macbeth, I.4

There is no vice so simple but assumes
Some mark of virtue on his outward parts.

The Merchant of Venice, III.2

He that but fears the thing he would not know
Has by instinct knowledge from others' eyes
That what he feared is chanced.

2 King Henry IV, I.1

A jest's prosperity lies in the ear
Of him that hears it, never in the tongue
Of him that makes it.

Love's Labour's Lost, V.2

Jealous souls ...
                are not ever jealous for the cause,
But jealous for they're jealous. It is a monster
Begot upon itself, born of itself.   *Othello*, III.4

                'Tis slander
Whose edge is sharper than the sword.

The Winter's Tale, II.2

                Other men
Put forth their sons to seek preferment out,
Some to the wars to try their fortune there,
Some to discover islands far away,
Some to the studious universities ...
Experience is by industry achieved.

The Two Gentlemen of Verona, I.3

Report of fashions in proud Italy,
Whose manners still our tardy apish nation
Limps after in base imitation.

King Richard II, II.1

We must supplant those rough, rug-headed kerns,
Which live like venom where no venom else
But only they have privilege to live.
[Ireland]   *Ibid*

What's a drunken man like, fool?
– Like a drowned man, a fool, and a madman: one draught above heat makes him a fool, the second mads him, and a third drowns him.

Twelfth Night, I.5

When we mean to build
We first survey the plot, then draw the model,
And when we see the figure of the house
Then must we rate the cost of the erection.

2 King Henry IV, I.3

Gold! yellow, glittering, precious gold …
Thus much of this will make black white, foul fair,
Wrong right, base noble, old young, coward valiant,
This yellow slave
Will knit and break religions …
place thieves
And give them title, knee and approbation
With senators on the bench.

Timon of Athens, IV.3

There are a kind of men so loose of soul
That in their sleeps will mutter their affairs.

Othello, III.3

True nobility is exempt from fear.

2 King Henry VI, IV.1

Such men as he be never at heart's ease
While they behold a greater than themselves.

Julius Caesar, I.2

… Men may construe things after their own fashion
Clean from the purpose of the things themselves.

Ibid

… When I tell him he hates flatterers
He says he does, being then most flattered.   *Ibid*, II.1

… Lowliness is young ambition's ladder …
But when he once attains the upmost round
He then unto the ladder turns his back,
Looks in the clouds, scorning the base degrees
By which he did ascend.   *Ibid*

Cowards die many times before their deaths,
The valiant never taste of death but once.   *Ibid*, II.2

The evil that men do lives after them,
The good is oft interrèd with their bones.   *Ibid*, III.1

Passion, I see, is catching.   *Ibid*

Between the acting of a dreadful thing
And the first motion all the interim is
Like a phantasma or a hideous dream.   *Ibid*, II.1

                    Virtue cannot live
Out of the teeth of emulation [envy].   *Ibid*, II.3

… A slight unmeritable man
Meet to be sent on errands.   *Ibid*, IV.1

There is a tide in the affairs of men
Which, taken at the flood, leads on to fortune;
Omitted, all the voyage of their life
Is bound in shallows and in miseries.   *Ibid*, IV.3

And oftentimes, to win us to our harm,
The instruments of darkness tell us truths,
Win us with honest trifles to betray us.   *Macbeth*, I.2

The labour we delight in physics pain.   *Ibid*, II.3

The season of all natures – sleep.   *Ibid*, III.4

Everyday Remarks

What men dare do! what men may do! what men daily
do, not knowing what they do!

Much Ado About Nothing, IV.1

… What we have we prize not to the worth
While we enjoy it; but, being lacked and lost,
Why, then we rack the value, then we find
The virtue that possession would not show us
While it was ours.   *Ibid*

… There was never yet philosopher
That could endure the toothache patiently.

Ibid, V.1

Everyone can master a grief but he that has it.

Ibid, III.1

O, what a world of vile ill-favoured faults
Looks handsome in three hundred pounds a year.

The Merry Wives of Windsor, III.4

How full of briars is this working-day world!

As You Like It, I.3

… the whining schoolboy with his satchel
And shining morning face, creeping like snail
Unwillingly to school.   *Ibid*, II.7

… as dry as the remainder biscuit
After a voyage.   *Ibid*

Time travels in divers paces with divers persons.

Ibid, III.2

Great griefs, I see, medicine the less.   *Cymbeline*, IV.2

        Though mean and mighty rotting
Together have one dust, yet reverence –
That angel of the world – doth make distinction
Of place between high and low.   *Ibid*

Every good servant does not all commands.   *Ibid*, V.1

When the blood burns how prodigal the soul
Lends the tongue vows.   *Hamlet*, I.3

Brevity is the soul of wit.   *Ibid*, II.2

When sorrows come they come not single spies
But in battalions.   *Ibid*, IV.5

Small have continual plodders ever won
Save base authority from others' books.

Love's Labour's Lost, I.1

'Tis an ill cook that cannot lick his own fingers.

Romeo and Juliet, IV.2

He that dies pays all debts.   *The Tempest*, III.2

Yet the first bringer of unwelcome news
Hath but a losing office, and his tongue
Sounds ever after as a sullen bell.   2 *King Henry IV*, I.1

Time is like a fashionable host,
That slightly shakes his parting guest by the hand,
And with his arms out-stretched as he would fly
Grasps in the comer: welcome ever smiles
And farewell goes out sighing.

Troilus and Cressida, III.3

O world! how apt the poor are to be proud.

Twelfth Night, III.1

Things sweet to taste prove in digestion sour.

King Richard II, I.3

'Tis merry in hall when beards wag all. *Ibid*, V.3

These fellows of infinite tongue that can rhyme
themselves into ladies' favours, they do always reason
themselves out again.

King Henry V, V.2

Unbidden guests
Are often welcomest when they are gone.

1 King Henry VI, II.2

There is a history in all men's lives
Figuring the nature of the times deceased:
The which observed a man may prophesy
With a near aim, of the main chance of things,
As yet not come to life.

2 King Henry IV, III.1

Characteristic Reflections

The better part of valour is discretion.

1 King Henry IV, V.4

Pleasure will be paid, one time or another.

Twelfth Night, III.4

Men shall deal unadvisedly sometimes
Which after-hours give leisure to repent.

King Richard III, IV.4

Heaven doth with us as we with torches do,
Not light them for themselves; for if our virtues
Did not go forth of us, 'twere all alike
As if we had them not.

Measure for Measure, I.1

When we our betters see bearing our woes
We scarcely think our miseries our foes.
Who alone suffers, suffers most in the mind.

King Lear, III.6

No man is the lord of anything –
Though in and of him there be much consisting –
Till he communicate his parts to others.
Nor doth he of himself know them for aught
Till he behold them formed in the applause
Where they're extended.

Troilus and Cressida, III.3

One touch of nature makes the whole world kin.

Ibid

Use every man after his own desert, and who should
'scape whipping? *Hamlet*, II.2

Have more than thou showest,
Speak less than thou knowest,
Lend less than thou owest,
Ride more than thou goest [walk],
Learn more than thou trowest [know],
Set [stake] less than thou throwest …
Leave thy drink and thy whore,
And keep in-a-door.
And thou shalt have more
Than two tens to a score. *King Lear*, I.4

O, it is excellent
To have a giant's strength, but it is tyrannous
To use it like a giant. *Measure for Measure*, II.2

But man, proud man,
Dressed in a little brief authority,
Most ignorant of what he's most assured …
Plays such fantastic tricks before high heaven
As make the angels weep. *Ibid*

Good name in man and woman
Is the immediate jewel of their souls. *Othello*, III.3

The quality of mercy is not strained,
It droppeth as the gentle rain from heaven
Upon the place beneath. It is twice blessed:
It blesseth him that gives and him that takes.
The Merchant of Venice, IV.1

In law, what plea so tainted and corrupt,
But, being seasoned with a gracious voice,
Obscures the show of evil? *Ibid*, III.2

Hath not a Jew eyes? hath not a Jew hands, organs,
dimensions, senses, affections, passions? fed with the
same food, hurt with the same weapons, subject to the
same diseases, healed by the same means, warmed and
cooled by the same winter and summer, as a Christian?

Ibid, III.1

It is a wise father that knows his own child.

Ibid

Truth will come to light; murder cannot be hid long.

Ibid

The Devil can cite Scripture for his purpose.   *Ibid*, I.3

A goodly apple rotten at the heart –
O, what a goodly outside falsehood hath!   *Ibid*

I like not fair terms and a villain's mind.   *Ibid*

They are as sick that surfeit with too much as they that
starve with nothing.

Ibid, I.2

If to do were as easy as to know what were good to do,
chapels had been churches, and poor men's cottages
princes' palaces.

Ibid

The web of our life is of a mingled yarn, good and ill
together. Our virtues would be proud if our faults
whipped them not; and our crimes would despair if they
were not cherished by our own virtues.

All's Well That Ends Well, IV.3

There's place and means for every man alive.　　*Ibid*

The flowery way that leads to the broad gate and the
great fire.　　*Ibid*, IV.5

　　　　Praising what is lost
Makes the remembrance dear.　　*Ibid*, V.3

　　　　　　We, ignorant of ourselves,
Beg often our own harms, which the wise powers
Deny us for our good. So find we profit
By losing of our prayers
　　　　　　　Antony and Cleopatra, II.1

Though it be honest it is never good
To bring bad news. Give to a gracious message
A host of tongues, but let ill tidings tell
Themselves when they be felt.　　*Ibid*, I.5

Ambition – the soldier's virtue.　　*Ibid*, III.1

　　　　　Man's judgments are
A parcel of their fortunes, and things outward
Do draw the inward quality after them
To suffer all alike.　　*Ibid*, III.11.

To business that we love we rise betime
And go to it with delight.　　*Ibid*

But when we in our viciousness grow hard –
O misery on it! – the wise gods seel our eyes;
In our own filth drop our clear judgments; make us
Adore our errors; laugh at us while we strut
To our confusion.　　*Ibid*

Your 'if' is the only peace-maker – much virtue in 'if'.
As You Like It, V.4

What custom wills in all things should we do it.
Coriolanus, II.3

To persèver
In obstinate condolement is a course
Of impious stubbornness; 'tis unmanly grief.　*Hamlet*, I.2

Give thy thoughts no tongue,
Nor any unproportioned thought his act.
Be thou familiar, but by no means vulgar.
The friends thou hast, and their adoption tried,
Grapple them to thy soul with hoops of steel ...
Give every man thine ear, but few thy voice.
Take each man's censure [opinion] but reserve thy
judgment.　　　　　　　　　　　　　　　　*Ibid*

There are more things in heaven and earth ...
Than are dreamt of in your philosophy.　　*Ibid*, V.1

That's an ill phrase, a vile phrase: 'beautified' is a vile
phrase.　　　　　　　　　　　　　　　　*Ibid*, II.2

There is nothing either good or bad but thinking makes
it so.　　　　　　　　　　　　　　　　　*Ibid*

The very substance of the ambitious is merely the
shadow of a dream.　　　　　　　　　　*Ibid*

With devotion's visage
And pious action we do sugar o'er
The devil himself.　　　　　　　　　　*Ibid*, III.1

Conscience doth make cowards of us all;
And thus the native hue of resolution
Is sicklied o'er with the pale cast of thought.   *Ibid*

Be thou as chaste as ice, as pure as snow, thou shalt not
escape calumny.   *Ibid*

What to ourselves in passion we propose,
The passion ending doth the purpose lose.

        Ibid, III.2

Our wills and fates do so contràry run
That our devices still [ever] are overthrown.   *Ibid*

            Whereto serves mercy
But to confront the visage of offence?   *Ibid*

Conceit in weakest bodies strongest works.   *Ibid*, III.4

            Diseases desperate grown
By desperate appliances are relieved,
Or not at all.   *Ibid*, IV.3

No place, indeed, should murder sanctuarise.

        Ibid, IV.7

Your dull ass will not mend his pace with beating.
        Ibid, V.1

There's a special providence in the fall of a sparrow. If it
be now, 'tis not to come; if it be not to come, it will be
now. If it be not now, yet it will come: the readiness is all.
        Ibid, V.2

Men at some time are masters of their fates –
The fault … is not in our stars
But in ourselves that we are underlings.

Julius Caesar, I.2

'Tis meet
That noble minds keep ever with their likes;
For who so firm that cannot be seduced?   *Ibid*

It seems to me most strange that men should fear,
Seeing that death, a necessary end,
Will come when it will come.   *Ibid*, II.2

That we shall die we know; 'tis but the time
And drawing days out that men stand upon.   *Ibid*, III.1

There are no tricks in plain and simple faith.   *Ibid*, III.4

For mine own part
I shall be glad to learn of noble men.   *Ibid*, IV.1

A friend should bear his friend's infirmities.   *Ibid*, IV.3

O hateful error, melancholy's child!
Why dost thou show to the apt thoughts of men
The things that are not?   *Ibid*, V.3

Striving to better, oft we mar what's well.

King Lear, I.4

To wilful men
The injuries that they themselves procure
Must be their schoolmasters.   *Ibid*, II.4

The art of our necessities is strange
That can make vile things precious.   *Ibid*, III.2

Take physic, pomp:
Expose thyself to feel what wretches feel.   *Ibid*, III.4

Keep thy foot out of brothels, thy hand out of plackets
[skirts], thy pen from lenders' books.   *Ibid*

As flies to wanton boys are we to the gods:
They kill us for their sport.   *Ibid*, IV.1

Wisdom and goodness to the vile seem vile;
Filths savour but themselves.   *Ibid*, IV.2

See how yon justice rails upon yon simple thief. ...
Change places and, handy-dandy, which is the justice,
which is the thief?   *Ibid*, IV.6

The worst is not,
So long as we can say, 'This is the worst.'   *Ibid*, IV.1

When we are born we cry, that we are come
To this great stage of fools.   *Ibid*, IV.6

Men must endure
Their going hence even as their coming hither:
Ripeness is all.   *Ibid*, IV.7

Who can be wise, amazed, temperate, and furious,
Loyal and neutral, in a moment? – No man.

Macbeth, II.3

There's daggers in men's smiles.   *Ibid*

Thriftless ambition, that wilt ravin [eat] up
Thine own life's means.   *Ibid*, II.4

Naught's had, all's spent,
When our desire is got without content.

Ibid, III.1

Things without all remedy
Should be without regard: what's done is done.

Ibid, III.2

Things bad begun make strong themselves by ill.

Ibid

If our virtues
Did not go forth of us, 'twere all alike
As if we had them not.

Measure for Measure, I.1

Spirits are not finely touched but to fine issues.

Ibid

Our doubts are traitors,
And make us lose the good we oft might win,
By fearing to attempt.   *Ibid*, I.4

The jury, passing on a prisoner's life,
May in the sworn twelve have a thief or two
Guiltier than him they try.   *Ibid*, II.1

Some rise by sin, and some by virtue fall.   *Ibid*

Most dangerous
Is that temptation that doth goad us on
To sin in loving virtue.   *Ibid*

Reason thus with life:
If I do lose thee I do lose a thing
That none but fools would keep: a breath thou art
Servile to all the skyey influences.   *Ibid*, III.1

The sense of death is most in apprehension.   *Ibid*

Superfluity comes sooner by white hairs, but
competency lives longer.   *The Merchant of Venice*, I.1

Men that hazard all
Do it in hope of fair advantages:
A golden mind stoops not to shows of dross.   *Ibid*, II.7

O, that estates, degrees, and offices
Were not derived corruptly, and that clear honour
Were purchased by the merit of the wearer!

Ibid, II.9

The ancient saying is no heresy:
'Hanging and wiving goes by destiny.'   *Ibid*

He is well paid that is well satisfied.   *Ibid*, IV.1

A victory is twice itself when the achiever brings home
full numbers.

Much Ado About Nothing, I.1

Patch grief with proverbs.   *Ibid*, V.1

In a false quarrel there is no true valour. *Ibid*

We cannot all be masters, nor all masters
Cannot be truly followed. *Othello*, I.1

I would not my unhoused free condition
Put into circumscription and confine
For the sea's worth. *Ibid*, I.2

To mourn a mischief that is past and gone
Is the next way to draw new mischief on.
Ibid, I.3

The robbed that smiles steals something from the thief.
Ibid

But words are words: I never yet did hear
That the bruisèd heart was piercèd through the ear.
Ibid

It is silliness to live when to live is torment; and then
have we a prescription to die when death is our
physician. *Ibid*

'Tis in ourselves that we are thus, or thus; our bodies are
our gardens, to which our wills are gardeners.
Ibid

Put money in thy purse. *Ibid*

The heavens forbid
But that our loves and comforts should increase
Even as our days do grow! *Ibid*, II.1

'Tis pride that pulls the country down. *Ibid*

Good wine is a good familiar creature if it be well used.
Ibid

Men should be what they seem. *Ibid*, III.3

He that filches from me my good name
Robs me of that which not enriches him
And makes me poor indeed. *Ibid*

Few love to hear the sins they love to act.
Pericles, I.1

O you gods,
Why do you make us love your goodly gifts,
And snatch them straight away?
Ibid, III.1

What's past is prologue. *The Tempest*, II.1

Misery acquaints a man with strange bedfellows.
Ibid, II.2

I wonder men dare trust themselves with men.
Timon of Athens, I.2

Nothing emboldens sin so much as mercy.
Ibid, III.5

Like madness is the glory of this life.
Ibid, I.2

O, the fierce wretchedness that glory brings us.

Ibid, IV.2

Come, and take choice of all my library
And so beguile thy sorrow.

Titus Andronicus, II.1

Young men, whom Aristotle thought
Unfit to hear moral philosophy.

Troilus and Cressida, II.2

Thus to persist
In doing wrong extenuates not wrong,
But makes it much more heavy.   *Ibid*

A plague of opinion! A man may wear it on both sides,
like a leather jerkin.   *Ibid,* III.3

Sometimes we are devils to ourselves
When we will tempt the frailty of our powers,
Presuming on their changeful potency.

Ibid, IV.4

The end crowns all,
And that old common arbitrator, Time,
Will one day end it.   *Ibid,* IV.5

Virtue that transgresses is but patched with sin; and sin
that amends is but patched with virtue.

Twelfth Night, I.5

And thus the whirligig of time brings in his revenges.

Ibid, IV.5

Home-keeping youth have ever homely wits.
The Two Gentlemen of Verona, I.1

New-made honour doth forget men's names.
King John, I.1

Courage mounteth with occasion.   *Ibid*, II.1

There is no virtue like necessity.
King Richard II, I.3

O God! that one might read the book of fate.
2 *King Henry IV*, III.1

A peace is of the nature of a conquest
For then both parties nobly are subdued,
And neither party loses.   *Ibid*, IV.2

Trust none;
For oaths are straw, men's faiths are wafer-cakes,
And hold-fast is the only dog.
King Henry V, II.3

Two may keep counsel, putting one away.
Romeo and Juliet, II.4

There is some soul of goodness in things evil,
Would men observingly distil it out.
Ibid, IV.1

'Tis a kind of good deed to say well –
And yet words are no deeds.
King Henry VIII, III.2

A peace above all earthly dignities:
A still and quiet conscience.

Ibid

Men's evil manners live in brass; their virtues
We write in water.

Ibid, IV.2

The gods are just, and of our pleasant vices
Make instruments to plague us.

King Lear, V.3

Religion

In religion
What damnèd error but some sober brow
Will bless it and approve it with a test?

The Merchant of Venice, III.2

Poor soul, the centre of my sinful earth ...
Why dost thou pine within and suffer dearth,
Painting thy outward walls so costly gay?
Why so large cost, having so short a lease?

Sonnet 146

So shalt thou feed on Death, that feeds on men,
And Death once dead, there's no more dying then.

Ibid

In those holy fields
Over whose acres walked those blessèd feet,
Which fourteen hundred years ago were nailed
For our advantage on the bitter cross.

1 King Henry IV, I.1

For Christian service and true chivalry,
As is the sepulchre in stubborn Jewry
Of the world's ransom, blessèd Mary's son.

King Richard II, II.1

'Tis not so above:
There is no shuffling, there the action lies
In his true nature, and we ourselves compelled,
Even to the teeth and forehead of our faults,
To give in evidence.

Hamlet, III.3

What is a man,
If his chief good and market of his time
Be but to sleep and feed? A beast, no more.

Ibid, IV.4

Sure he that made us with such large discourse,
Looking before and after, gave us not
That capability and god-like reason
To fust in us unused.   *Ibid*

Why, all the souls that were were forfeit once,
And He that might the vantage best have took
Found out the remedy. How would you be
If He, which is the top of judgment, should
But judge you as you are?

Measure for Measure, II.2

Mercy is above this sceptred sway,
It is enthronèd in the hearts of kings,
It is an attribute to God himself,
And earthly power doth then show likest God's
When mercy seasons justice.

The Merchant of Venice, IV.1

If when you make your prayers
God should be so obdurate as yourselves
How would it fare with your departed souls?

2 *King Henry VI*, IV.7

They say miracles are past.

All's Well That Ends Well, II.3

For the life to come I sleep out the thought of it.

The Winter's Tale, IV.2